Table of Content

1.	The Power of a Peaceful Mind	01
2.	Be At Peace with The Decisions You Make	07
3.	Maintaining Peace with Those Around You	12
4.	Never Compare Yourself to Others	20
5.	5 Ways to Remain Consistently Peaceful	27
6.	5 Ways to Avoid Overthinking	33
7.	10 Ways to Practice Peace	39
8.	Be At Peace with The Past	45
9.	Create An Environment of Peace in Your Life	52
10.	Cultivate An Attitude of Peace and Calm	59
11.	How To Develop Inner Tranquility	66
12.	How To Wake Up Peacefully in The Morning	71
13.	Introspection: The Key to Inner Peace	77
14.	No One Else Is Responsible	85
15.	Peace Affirmations That Work	92
16.	Say NO to Some Things	99
17.	Stop Worrying About What Others Think	105

Chapter 1

THE POWER OF A PEACEFUL MIND

There are things about life I wish I learned early. One of them is the importance of peace of mind. Growing up, I was a softie. I allowed even the smallest of things to get into me and reside freely in my head. I gave room to sad events without even noticing or caring about what it was doing to me. I remember how I cried about the passing away of my grandfather and my sister for years. I have been self-conscious for the longest time. I will never forget how, until recent years, I have been so much concerned about what I did not have yet. I have also carried the heavy burden of regretting missed opportunities and wasted ones. What I learned from all these was that they did nothing but take away my peace. So, on top of everything I had experienced and was suffering from, I added tears and anxiety.

Being in this state of mind (anxiety and sadness) also gave permanence to all those issues that led to it. I could not fight or think of myself as capable to win the war. Negativity clouded my mind and I was going round in circles. It was when I made a conscious decision to be happy that I started seeing a difference in my life. It changed my opinion of myself, and you will not believe how much improvement I've seen in my life as a result.

If you are suffering from depression, anxiety, or any kind of stress, you are not alone. A majority of people have gone through it. But, those who manage to turn things around do so because they make happiness a goal and choose it every day. For the record, if you do not learn to be mentally stable, nothing will ever satisfy you. You will reach your goals, want more, and consequently feel as though all your other achievements are nothing. A peaceful mind can do the following for you:

1.   It keeps you clear-headed – a peaceful mind functions better. Worries can distract you as they tend to stay at the back of your head and pop up anytime. This is how you get tasks mixed up, things pass you by without you noticing, and important things are forgotten. In other terms, you focus better when you are at peace.

2.   It is easier to fight negativity – when you have a peaceful mind, you are not easily affected by any form of negativity. The fact that you have a clear head makes it easier to analyze situations and understand them better instead of taking them at face value and letting them consume you. For example, where someone chooses to be mean to you, you can try and imagine their stressful work environment or how bad their own situation could be instead of assuming that there is something wrong with you and you don't have much value as a human being. You can easily survive different situations.

3.   It makes you confident – you accept and are content with who you are and just want to keep growing. You don't have inner voices fighting for attention concerning what you can or cannot do. It is easier for people who accept their level of intelligence, skills, or looks among other things to stand tall, stay focused, and want to do more with their lives. Failing to accept who you are will always give you a reason to hard and, it makes it easier for other people to use it against you.

4.   It helps you live your life to the fullest – being at peace makes it easier for you to give attention to all areas of your life and balance things up where the lack thereof will make you focus more on the one thing that you assume will make you happy. You learn to appreciate every single part of your life.

5.   You are in a position to create genuine relationships – when you are not at peace, some of the relationships you form are driven by pressure, the need to be relevant, and desperation among other things. Such relationships are often based on short-term goals and do not have a strong foundation. The involved parties tolerate instead of loving and respecting each other. The weaker tends to be used and there is often backstabbing involved.

6.   You are not scared to try things out – lack of inner peace can downplay you in various ways especially where there is self-consciousness or self-doubt. You easily dismiss ideas and opportunities because you judge yourself and conclude that you are not worthy or you do not qualify before others get a chance to share their thoughts with you. In fact, you are even scared that they will confirm what you have always thought of yourself. What if others see you differently? Those who are at peace understand that the actual loss is not trying because you lose a chance to discover more about life and yourself.

7.   The past has no hold on you – the ability to let go of the past frees you from it. You are then able to focus on the present and the future without worrying about the past and its experiences. Many have failed to work with other people or share ideas with them because of what happened in the past. Some have even given up on romantic relationships. A peaceful mind allows you to keep on giving life another chance.

Chapter 2

BE AT PEACE WITH THE DECISIONS YOU MAKE

American motivational author Louise Hay once said "No person, no place, and no thing has any power over us, for 'we' are the only thinkers in our mind. When we create peace, harmony, and balance in our minds, we will find it in our lives." Such a profound quote capturing the superiority of our mindset and thoughts. Everything that governs our actions is a manifestation of what we're thinking. It is not spoken enough about the limitless things we can achieve if we have an active mindset. A self-aware conscious mind. A positive peaceful mindset.

My father taught me something crucial at a young age. He taught me that every time I look in the mirror, I should remind myself of this thing; He said, 'each day, look into your eyes through a mirror and remind yourself two important things. You're your biggest competition, and you're also your worst enemy'. In this short lesson, he was illuminating the same lesson from madam Louise's quote. Certainly, no person and no place have power over us except ourselves. If we can overcome our worst enemy, 'ourselves', nothing else and no one else can stand in our way. Our lives are indeed our responsibility. If we're the drivers of our destinations, we make the decisions. We decide on the thoughts that we allow for our reaction. By so doing, we're at peace with every decision we make in our lives because it is ours to make. We understand that what is meant for us will find us. Failures and disappointment are not the ends of the world. This is being at peace with our choices.

The biggest hurdle to achieving this peace is setting a balance within our minds. A place of unwavering thoughts. Where our yes becomes a yes and a no is a no. This is a mindset that stays undefiled by the outcome of our decisions. Whether the result is favorable or not to the circumstance or agenda, this is the mindset that stays optimistic. It says, 'I may not get it now, but I'll keep on trying my best. I can deal with the results because it is my life and it is my responsibility. I am in control. No matter the outcome, I can try again and make it better. It is one thing to know what you want to achieve. It's another thing to put to practice.

Inner peace is built and nurtured from within like a muscle. It is what we're feeding our minds and inner beings every day that is manifesting into the decisions we're choosing to make. Here's a short story to further elucidate on the matter. Jane and Sarah are both on a weight loss journey. From the onlookers, Jane seems to understand why she needs to lose weight. She's surrounding herself with a team of ladies who are on the same agenda. She's sticking to her diet plan and workout routines accordingly. Sarah on the other hand seems to be having a different approach from Jane. She has no diet plan or workout routine. She's pretty much throwing curveballs as she goes. One evening, Jane and Sarah decided to go out with some friends for dinner. They both ended up making some unhealthy eating decisions that night. The question then is, who do you think was more at peace with the decisions they made that evening?

We could be quick to judge that Sarah probably woke up feeling a bit miserable the next morning; But, again, inner peace is per individual. Some people find their peace, from living in the present moment. They live their lives as the man who knows there's no tomorrow. He lives knowing that the next moment is not guaranteed to him. He finds fulfillment in small daily routines and successes. Other people find peace in living a well-thought life. They plan and work for tomorrow and the day after tomorrow and the next seasons to come. These two men are both living their truths. The only difference between the latter from the former man is their belief or mindset. We should know our truth. We should be honest with ourselves so that we're at peace with our different realities. Our mindset creates our reality. When our reality resonates with our scale of satisfaction, we find inner peace and fulfillment. We all have different scales of satisfaction. To one man little is enough. To another man little is not good enough. Finding an inner balance to that scale is what determines how satisfied we'll be with the decisions we're making.

John F. Kennedy said, 'Peace is a daily, a weekly, a monthly process, gradually changing opinions, slowly eroding old barriers, quietly building new structures." Not only are we going to learn how to find peace, but we're also going to learn ways to consistently remain peaceful through each day'.

Chapter 3

MAINTAINING PEACE WITH THOSE AROUND YOU

If possible, to the best of your ability, live at peace with everyone.

In a world where chaos is the order of the day, it is our responsibility to maintain peace in our environments. To expect peace to come from external sources is to set ourselves up for a disgruntled existence. The greatest source of peace in your life comes from within you. When you have inner peace, it makes it easier to deal with difficult situations that arise. You relate better with those who surround you when you approach every situation with a sense of calm instead of anger and frustration.

Peace does not imply the absence of trouble. To expect that adopting a state of peace will eradicate difficulties in our lives is to delude ourselves. Life is full of trials. Every day we fight different battles that make peace seem impossible. People try our patience. Workloads put a lot of pressure on our backs. Negative situations pop up. We lose loved ones. Such is the way of life.

We can, however, control our reaction to adversity because losing our temper or whining about our situation will change nothing. It builds negativity, and the results are detrimental to our well-being. Being negative will only damage our mental state, disrupt our health, and affect how we relate with others. The only thing that can help us come out of such vicious cycles is adopting a peaceful demeanor when hard times hit.

When confronted with difficulties, the first instinct is to panic and let your imagination run wild with thoughts of how you will not make it out. Think back on the times you hit a rough patch in your life. It could be the moment you lost your job or a bad financial season in your business. It could be the first break-up or losing a close relative. What drove your reactions then? Possibly how you responded to the situation was irrational because you were angry, anxious, or afraid that you would not survive that painful season. That is the default human response to trouble. A different approach would be to adopt peace as the primary force behind your reactions.

Peace allows you to deal with the circumstances you face differently. It allows you to process what you are going through calmly. Peace accepts the negative situation as temporary, not as a death sentence. It gives you the option to deal with what is before you more rationally.

People will step on your toes- even those you love. Being at loggerheads with everyone who rubs you the wrong way will drain you of the energy you are better off investing in improving your life. The best way to handle it would be to let peace lead. It is possible to maintain peace with the people around you.

How to maintain peace.

Practice patience.

It is easy to let frustration rule your dealings with others who do not seem to be on the same wavelength as you. Whether you feel right, or smarter, more knowledgeable; or whether you have more experience than others, there is no need to lose your patience. Come to the other person's level. Listen to them. Try to understand them. Never belittle them. Be patient enough to walk them through things if they do not seem to catch on. Patience goes a long way to improve our relations with others.

Be compassionate.

We all struggle with things we may not be open to sharing with others around us. Our minds are riddled with internal conflicts before we even engage with other people. Do not add mental stress to another if you can avoid it. Empathy goes a long way in avoiding conflict. Do not respond to anger with anger. It solves nothing. If you sense someone's frustration, do not aggravate them. Give them room to cool off before you take up any issues with them. It goes a long way in promoting peace if we all understand each other.

Be more forgiving.

Humans are prone to making mistakes. No one is perfect. There is no need to nail anyone to the cross for an error in judgment. The best way to bring peace to their world and yours is to forgive them. Holding on to their mistake and lording it over them every time will bring tension and ruin relations. Forgive them and move on.

Holding on to conflict and confrontation will harm you. There are certain matters that you can let go. Be the bigger person.

We should also be more forgiving with ourselves when we do wrong. Beating ourselves up over an incident will create a lot of turmoil. Forgiving ourselves brings peace.

Be gracious in your speech.

People fight fire with fire. When you use accusatory and offensive language, conflict will arise. Be firm in your correction without disrespecting anyone.

Tolerance.

When we try to change other people into what we want them to be, we are creating room for conflict to erupt. People are unique. We should accept them for who they are. We should tolerate other people's differences because we will certainly not always agree with their choices and vice versa. Tolerance is the path to harmony.

Agree to disagree.

Arguments will always come. Our differences in opinion cause us to have different perceptions on matters such as politics, ethics, and so on. Instead of pushing your opinion on another, accept

that they have a right to theirs as well. We do not have to agree to get along.

It is possible to maintain peace with others around you. All you need to do is to stop yourself from dictating your interactions with people in your sphere.

It is not possible to love everyone, but we can surely co-exist in peace. Treat every person as you would want to be treated.

So then, let us pursue what makes for peace and mutual up-building.

Chapter 4

NEVER COMPARE YOURSELF TO OTHERS

No man is an island. We all are part of a community made up of different characters whose lives can be interdependent. As such, we cannot help but notice how much and what others are doing around us. Some inspire us while others serve as examples of what not to try. It is normal to admire people or just watch them and think to yourself what it would mean to you if you lived a life similar to theirs or better. It's probably harmless even. However, you should know that you have lost it when you start comparing yourself to those people, even those who inspire you.

The most common ways in which people compare themselves to others include:

a)   Having a role model or admiring someone else's life so much that you try to follow their every step to get what they have or to where they are

b)   Using your peers' achievements as a standard by which you measure your success or failure

Having a role model does not mean that you should do things the exact way s/he did to get where s/he is. It does not mean that you have to be like that person in every possible way. You can be yourself and still achieve the same things if you play your part well in whatever task needs your attention. I'm sure we all would hate to live in monotonous societies where everyone gets what they dream of at the exact time or age their predecessors did. It sucks the fun out of life because of the predictability of each step. I cannot imagine what that would do to creativity, exclusivity, and growth in other areas of life.

When it comes to peers' achievement, I won't lie that it is easy to feel as if you are way too behind and haven't done well with your time regardless of the effort you have continued to put in whatever you do. It is also easy to feel proud of how you seem to be doing better than everyone else. Whatever your case could be, it is important to remember that things aren't always as they seem and every individual is running their own race. Success is not only measured by the amount of wealth you have accumulated over time. Judging from your past and where you want to go, what other victories –small or big- have you had? How much have you grown socially, mentally, and spiritually among other things? Have you set a strong foundation for the future you want? All these are crucial and the lack thereof can easily make you and your financial value incompatible.

Therefore, always keep this in mind: the only people you should compare yourself to are your old self, the present, and the person you want to be in future. Are you better than the person you were yesterday and have you forgiven yourself for your past weaknesses? Are you doing your best to make the present memorable and fruitful? Are you working hard enough and are your goals and strategies what is required for you to be the person you envision yourself to be in future? From the way I see it, we have just too much on our plate to be concerned about what others have achieved especially because we do not have full details about why they do what they are doing and how, truly, they are doing it. Below are more reasons why we should never compare ourselves to others:

1.   You will become miserable – people are not waiting for you to catch up yet catching up is the only thing that can make you feel better. You will then be forced to try and speed up or take shortcuts which can worsen the situation. Every failure will bring unbearable pain because you are all about outcomes and have no/less interest in learning. You will not find inner peace.

2.   You could limit yourself – other people's failures or feeling like you are doing better than others can cause you to relax. You become content with staying at the top instead of pushing yourself to do the best possible. With that kind of mentality, you hardly collaborate with others because you do not want them to 'know your secret'. You do not learn as much as you would if you were not comparing yourself to others.

3.   You lose confidence – comparing yourself to those who are seemingly doing well can make you feel like a failure. You feel as if the reason you have 'not done enough' is that you are not good or smart enough.

4.   You ruin relationships – people who like comparing themselves to others easily ruin relationships with friends, family, and colleagues too. They have the mentality that if they achieved certain things at a certain time, anyone who is failing to do the same is not working hard enough. They tend to be controlling and have no time to consider what the next person is going through.

5.   You will lose sense of purpose – when you constantly concern yourself about how much others are doing or how good you think it is, it is easier for you to lose direction. You try to fit in and you do just about anything that can help you achieve a goal regardless of whether it is aligned to your purpose. You end up living another person's life.

6.   You easily make enemies – comparing yourself to others arouses a spirit of competition. Anyone with that kind of attitude does not need a reason to have enemies. The fact that they are found with other people in the same room automatically means they have to fight for whatever spot and be recognized.

Chapter 5

5 WAYS TO REMAIN CONSISTENTLY PEACEFUL

We all have days when we feel like the universe is pushing our red buttons. Days when our inner-balance scales are getting tipped. When we feel we don't have it all under control. Just one failure would trigger a spiral that goes back to eleven years ago when we fell off a bike. That reminded us of our childhood pet Lucky who was hit by a car. We start thinking 'why is everything not going on my way'. Self-doubt and all the negative emotions sneak in, and we struggle to turn that red button off.

We all have been down this road. No matter how at peace we may be with ourselves, at times, our environments can bring in the negativity that can disrupt our peace of mind. The mind can easily be thrown into disarray if our sub-conscience is not properly cultured. So often we encounter misleading thoughts that alter our decisions and way of thinking, even our personalities. As the saying goes,' the same things we feed our souls and spirit, are the same things that manifest out of it'.   To remain at peace, we need to consistently train the mind. We must understand how to calm our souls and create a peaceful aura around us.

1.   Guide your peace

We could never find peace if we're constantly at war with ourselves. One of my favorite speakers Joyce Meyer says people should stop upsetting themselves. She explains that there are certain people who often speak negatively about themselves. They provoke their peace. They have conversations with people they know they'll say something to upset them. They are always prepared for disappointment. They tell themselves that nothing is ever good enough for them. They can never be satisfied with anything in life. They don't recognize the small victories they make. For some, they go on to set unrealistic expectations. Instead of guiding their inner peace, they are constantly at battle with their thoughts.

However, to consistently be peaceful, we need to learn how to guide our peace. How does one achieve this? Firstly, by shying away from the things and people that trigger and upsets our calm. A lesson to remember, we must be gentle and kind to ourselves. We should truly love ourselves first before we can accept the world around us.

2.   Create routines and enjoyable habits

When we are doing something that we enjoy, our minds are far from everything that may trigger us. We are most calm and at peace with ourselves. So, find activities that keep you calm, that helps maintain your inner peace. Listen to music, paint, read a book, the list is endless. Anything that can take your mind away from your worries is essential. When we indulge in activities we enjoy, we stimulate our happy hormones and this reduces stress. Feelings of anxiety and distress will be replaced with joy and peace.

3.   Meditation and Reaffirmation

Meditation can be a useful tool to stay connected to our inner selves. It promotes emotional health and enhances self-awareness and emotional balance. According to Deepak Chopra, "meditation is not a way of making your mind quiet. It is a way of entering into the quiet that is already there – buried under the 50000 thoughts the average person thinks every day." Words of affirmation build our fighting spirit. They set our minds to think positively. What we hear and tell ourselves constantly, will eventually become part of us. However,

Affirmations are powerful if we can believe in what we're saying. They resonate with our truth. We cannot affirm something while thinking 'that is entirely impossible for me'. The goal is to let our affirmations and positive thinking be entwined with our subconscious mindset. This will help us find peace in situations where we need it the most.

4.   Acknowledge victories

If we focus more on what we didn't get and where we failed, we miss acknowledging what we've already achieved. This will continuously stress us. Counting the eggs that cracked as losses stops us from counting the chicks that hatched as wins. I find it soothing to my soul to have time to sit and reflect on all the things I've achieved in my life. Whenever I feel the storms coming in and suffocating my judgment, I take a pause. I sit somewhere peaceful with no distractions and list down my goals and all the things I achieved. This reminds me that my worries are only temporary. It shows me that with a little patience and endurance, I could still take my wins. My heart becomes at ease, and I'm motivated to fight.

The things of the past are meant to stay in the past. Failures of yesterday are not supposed to obstruct our tomorrow's progress.

5.   Develop peaceful relationships

Some people just radiate optimism. Conversing with them feels like burdens are being lifted off our shoulders. These are the kind of people we want to be around whenever possible. People who can build us up and not pull us down with them. We should also learn to be accepting of others. It is stressful always wishing to change others' opinions or behaviors. If we focus on ourselves first, we'll be able to help others later. In Ralph

5 Ways to Avoid Overthinking

Overthinking is a result of one of the most complex emotions we must deal with as humans and that emotion is FEAR. Fear cripples, it steals your peace and leaves you down and out and this is even before anything has happened. Fear as some have elucidated to mean False Evidence Appearing Real, cripples us by making us worry about something that has not even happened yet. Our minds go into overdrive worrying and fearing something that has not even taken place. This drives us into overthinking every minute detail, pondering as to what can go wrong and the many ways it can go wrong. Here are some nuggets on how to avoid overthinking and reclaim peace over your life.

1.   Live one day at a time.

We have the tendency to think and plan about the future so much that we forget that the present is happening. By relegating taking care of ourselves now and worrying about the future, we mess it all up before it even happens. Understand that tomorrow is a gift that none of us are promised, so make the most of the time you have today. Going into overdrive thinking about the future does not in any way secure it because the things that will happen tomorrow cannot be controlled. To avoid overthinking, take each day as it comes, see the gifts in what you already have, and trust that things will work out eventually in the end.

2.   Act on your worries.

Overthinking also happens in relationships. We worry about what the other person is thinking, and we stress ourselves trying to figure out a way either to make things right or just to know where their mind is. The best way to know anything is to find out. Communication will inform you if there is anything to worry about at all. Find out from the person how they feel and take things from there. Overthinking is crippling, most of us just take in the suffering without taking action on the things that are putting our minds into overdrive. Make that call to get clarification, send that email, that text, do whatever you can to try and set your mind at ease instead of just stewing over things.

3.   Focus on what you can control

If there is anything that always reminds us that we are not in control in a situation where our peace and stillness are dependent on someone else. When you overthink, sometimes nothing can be done about the situation, and this eats away at us further. As difficult as it is, you must focus on what you can control. You can control your actions, and what happens around you. Focus on those things that bring you peace and stillness. In some situations, no matter how much we mull over them, there is no solution in overthinking, rather focus on those things that you can control.

4.   Face your fears

As mentioned earlier, overthinking is fueled by your fears. For as long as you do not deal with your fears, they will drive you up the wall into overthinking. Most people have the fear of abandonment; thus, they refuse to face the other person fearing that they will be abandoned. Overthinking will kick in, robbing them of their joy and peace, and no matter how much they overthink the solution can only be found once they confront their fear. Ignoring your fears or brushing them off will not bring peace. The issue can like dormant for a while but when something triggers you, you are right back where you started. So, the best way to avoid overthinking is to deal with your fears before they deal with you.

5.   Find ways to unwind

Overthinking devastatingly affects our mental health. It can make you question your decisions, and you can forget who you are at the core. It is important to find ways to remind yourself of who you are so that overthinking does not become your identity. People have different ways to unwind and remind themselves of who they are, others read scripture, others meditate, go to the gym, speak affirmations, run, yoga there are several ways available. No way is better than the other, just pick one that will remind you of who you are so that you can think clearly and make sound decisions that you are proud of. Your mental health is just as important as your physical health. Overthinking can lead to more serious conditions such as anxiety, panic attacks, and depression. Thus, nipping overthinking in the bud, choosing the way of peace can improve your overall lifestyle.

The solutions suggested here are by no means comprehensive and they are not easy to do, but anything worthwhile in life takes effort. When you put the effort into your mental wellness you are guaranteed to lead a peaceful life. This does not mean that you will not face challenges, but that you will not be defeated by them because you know how to avoid the trap of overthinking.

10 Ways to Practice Peace

1.   Loving yourself

"Love your neighbor as you love yourself." This is indeed one of the most profound wisdom that can abundantly nourish people's lives when applied correctly. It stems from the understanding that you cannot give what you do not have. The relationship you have with yourself will influence all other relationships you will have, be it with family, friends, your significant other, or strangers. It is impossible to love others well without learning to love yourself first. It is also impossible for others to love you or treat you as you ought to be treated until you learn to take the lead and decide to love yourself first.

2. Forgiveness

When one does not forgive others, the same fate, unfortunately, befalls them with their spiritual relationships. To not be judged, we too should judge not. Forgiveness is choosing to accept what has happened and not letting it continue to have power over you. Unforgiveness robs you day and night of your peace and joy. Forgiveness allows you to let go and no longer be a prisoner of your past. It leads to progress and sustainable peace.

3. Thinking before you act

Impulsive behavioral patterns often have serious negative consequences. When angry people often say words they do not mean which can cost them their peace and so much more. Rather than acting on the urge to immediately react when things happen, it is wise to take some time. Give yourself time to understand the situation better before reacting. Breath, think, ask questions to ensure you understood correctly, then respond from a place of maturity.

4. Avoid procrastination

Do not procrastinate to do things tomorrow that can be done today or earlier. Procrastination leads to mental exhaustion as the weight of remembering the deadlines and more things that need to be done will keep weighing you down. Just practice saying no to distractions and do what needs to be done on time.

5. Conflict management

Conflict is inevitable, no matter where you go. Running away from it or pretending that nothing phases you is a recipe for peace deprivation. Take the time to learn how to peacefully address conflict with mutual respect. Choose a suitable time and location to do so. Speak from your heart with logic, love, and consideration when addressing things. Listen compassionately when someone else is sharing their side of the story. End the conversation with a healthy consensus and way forward for both parties involved. Learn to practice sincerely apologizing when you are the one in the wrong.

6. Discover your identity and purpose, dare to live it!

The two most important days in a person's life is the day you are born and the day you discover why. It is no doubt one of the biggest tragedies to have lived most of your life not knowing who your Creator created you to be and why. Wholeness and peace are attained when we become enlightened about who we truly are and why we were created. It is hence important to take the time to acquire that knowledge from your maker to be at peace in this life. Every created thing has a designer, to know it well and use it to the best of its ability, one has to ask the designer and read the manual then use it for what it was made for. If we can easily do that for our phones, laptops, home appliances, why can't we do it for ourselves?

7. Prioritize your health and wellness

Sickness can be avoided by actively creating a lifestyle that includes good eating habits, practicing good interpersonal skills, exercising, drinking lots of alkaline warm water, having a good rest amongst many other things. You cannot buy life once it is gone. Prioritize your health and wellness.

8. Meditation

Meditation helps you to be mindful. It helps you to assimilate deep into your consciousness norms, values, lessons that you need to live by and avoid living a reactive life. There are so many benefits of meditation that you can learn and apply to attain peace.

9. Paradigm Shift

A paradigm shift is consciously deciding to have a fundamental shift in your approach to life. It is getting rid of wrong perceptions, limiting beliefs, and stereotypes that are like a program that used to run your life to the extent that it would happen even subconsciously. Replace negative beliefs with positive beliefs and affirmations and choose to act from a place of mindfulness and maturity.

10. Cultivating good relationships through spreading a culture of peace

Connection is a primary human basic need. Without good relationships with people, life becomes a battlefield and a burden. It is important to practice a culture of peaceful coexistence when living with people. Putting effort to understand others and serving them. Adding value to others is important. A life selfishly lived only haunts the owner. Do good to others as you would want done unto you. Cultivate an attitude of gratitude. Tackle challenges one day at a time, you cannot solve all problems in one day. Dare to celebrate life and honor yourself with the gift of peace!

Ego says, "Once everything falls into place, I'll feel peace." Spirit says, "Find your peace, and then everything will fall into place."- Marianne Williamson

Be At Peace with The Past

"Peace begins with you." - Manhee Lee. A good tree bears good fruit, a bad tree bears bad fruit. We can either be happy with the good fruit we see in the various aspects of our lives or be saddened by the bad fruit we are yielding in the other aspects of our lives. The ideal reality we wish to see is us being like a healthy tree planted by the streams of water, which yields its fruit every month, in which the leaves never wither and whatever it does prosper. However, in many cases to attain that reality is often difficult, how then do we make our lives become like a good tree which bears good fruit in season? How does our past influence us attaining this goal?

Focus on the tree, not the fruit!

To become like a good tree that bears good fruit in our present and future times, one needs to come to an understanding that the outcome of your life today has been largely shaped by you. The decisions you made. The ideologies you chose to live by. The events that happened in your past shaped who you became today. How you learned to adapt and respond to situations in your environment and so much more.

In the present, all we see is usually the fruit of what your past generated your present reality to be. We look at our relationship's history, health, goals, socioeconomic status and we are often not happy with what we see. The immediate response is usually blaming external factors or people instead of focusing on nourishing the roots of the tree with self-care. Yes, the past may have exposed you to harsh adverse conditions that led you to be like an unhealthy tree producing unhealthy fruit, however, to live with bitterness and resentment over that reality will only lead to the tree remaining in that unhealthy situation and eventually dying.

When we focus on accepting that what happened to this tree happened and yes it was not right, however, I will move on to attending to the needs of the tree now, we start to see positive change. Every well-nourished tree automatically bears good fruit. Hence, let our primary focus be attending to the root of the problem rather than focusing on treating the symptoms. Be at peace with the past and do what you can now to create the reality you desire.

Dealing with past trauma

Almost everyone went through different kinds of trauma, be it physical, emotional, verbal, domestic, or childhood abuse and trauma. Most of our needs we expect our primary caregivers to cater for us are sadly often unmet in most people's lives. This leaves a generation like we see today and in past decades of people struggling with all sorts of invisible yet visible problems.

These include struggles with an identity crisis, self-worth, low self-esteem, constantly not feeling good enough, perfectionism paralysis, self-sabotage, imposter syndrome and so much more internal turmoil that throws our outer experiences into a roller coaster of chaotic experiences. Ultimately, we can see that even though we are alive in the present, we are also very much attached to the past in a negative way that is no longer serving us. One will be entangled in all sorts of destructive coping mechanisms that often do not work; in most cases, they lead one to re-living their painful past.

Face the past, carry the lesson with you forever but not the past!

To evolve into becoming the best versions of ourselves we all need to face challenges. The attitude in which we embrace is what will determine whether our past will make or break us. To be at peace with the past one must consciously decide to actively attain that peace. The following insights help aid one to finally be at peace with their past.

Awareness:

Awareness is the art of being mindful and enlightened about a particular thing. In this case, taking time to understand our past will help one to understand their present reality and take the lessons necessary. It frees one from being entangled in toxic behavioral patterns due to one's adverse past experiences.

An example of this can be someone who finds themselves in repeated toxic relationships with partners who end up trampling on them and not serving their needs. This pattern could be due to perhaps growing up not learning how to love yourself. As a result, that person's past influences the individual to have dysfunctional relationships because they lack self-worth and esteem, hence it ends up affecting every other relationship that person has until they decide to learn to be aware of their past. Once one has the correct diagnosis of the past, they can apply the relevant remedies in the present and be at peace with their past, no longer hostage to re-living the same painful experiences in the present

Forgiveness, letting go, and moving on:

Forgiveness is giving up the hope that the past could be any different. Accepting that it has happened to you. This does not mean accepting that it was okay for it to happen. It simply entails accepting that life will not always go the way we want it to and choosing to acknowledge that fact.

Letting go of the hurt allows one to no longer be a prisoner of the past. It allows one to move on. Letting go is empowering and helps you be at peace and reserve more energy for investing in your present. Letting go is essential to be at peace with your past. This way one undoubtedly takes back their power they would have given away to the past events or people still causing them to suffer.

Do not cheat on your future with your past, it's over. Choose peace, you can do it!

Create An Environment of Peace In Your Life Problems

If there is anyone who owes you a peaceful life, it is you. If you are waiting for anyone else to come to your rescue and make life better for you, then you will wait forever. It sounds harsh but the sooner we come to terms with that truth the better. Name any other person who understands your pain, your choices, your needs, your dreams, and everything about you better than yourself. Name anyone who can control your mind and actions better than you do.

If you are asking yourself about the relevance of all these things to the topic, the answer still is:

we have so much control over what happens in our lives than we realize. We know exactly what makes us cry or smile and the thoughts that pull us back or keep us going. Therefore, we have the power to control the greater part of our environment. Where we are not in any position to control what happens around us, we at least can program our minds to deal with it. Creating an environment of peace means creating a safe space for you to run to when faced with challenges. It is not the same as creating a fake world of happiness or running away from problems as these only leave your issues with no one to attend to them and they keep piling up. Rather, it is about your ability to remain sane and at peace as you face your problems head-on.

Why is it important to create an environment of peace in your life problems and how can you do it?

1.   It is almost impossible to avoid problems. Where you avoid creating them yourself, someone else or nature can throw them at you and in most cases, when you least expect it. Unless you have learned to create an environment of peace, you will most likely spend your short years of life miserable and/or running away from your problems.

2.   Remaining calm in your life problems puts you in a better position to find the best possible solutions where the opposite will make you look for an easy escape without considering other consequences. You feel as though you are in a desperate position which blurs your view and pushes you to do the first thing that comes to your mind. This can go on to create more problems for you. Peace helps you stay positive.

3.   Creating an environment of peace in life problems keeps you from magnifying your issues. Your problems may not be too bad or without an easy solution, but your lack of peace can cause you to feel helpless and make you panic.

4.   Failing to find peace in your problems makes you vulnerable to manipulations and other schemes from predators. Some people are always ready to exploit those in need and if you do not stay calm you could easily become a willing prey.

5. Calmly approaching life situations makes you stronger and wiser. You get to know how much you can take as you learn lessons on how to deal not only with problems but with other people too. You get to understand what to or what not to do to avoid facing the same problem in future. More importantly, bravely facing situations makes you brave enough to face more challenging ones.

6. Learning to be at peace when facing problems preserves relationships and keeps you from making enemies. Remaining peaceful even where you feel you were wronged can keep you from ruining people and your relationships. You learn to handle issues calmly and choose words wisely. You create strong and meaningful partnerships too.

7. A peaceful environment in life problems makes you resilient. Obstacles cannot stop you from getting what you want because of your ability to remain sane in situations that would normally break you and instill fear in you. As mentioned previously, that gives you a clear view of things, and not making rushed decisions helps you make calculated moves that can keep you moving towards your dreams. Success will be your companion.

Below is how you can create an environment of peace;

Build mental strength – this is just as important as physical strength, if not more important. Mental strength allows you to be in control of your thoughts including how you process external factors that affect how you view yourself and life in general. You build mental strength by feeding your mind the right things and leaving no room for any form of negativity, among other things. Stay positive.

Build healthy relationships – stay away from toxic people who will make you doubt yourself and the beauty of life. Build strategic relationships that align with who you want to be and surround yourself with supportive people who will also know how to give constructive criticism.

Learn to be content – contentment will help you stay in your lane. It protects you from peer pressure and living other people's dreams while it helps you appreciate who you are and what you have. However, this does not mean that you should dream small. Instead, it means that as you dream big and continue to work hard, do not be tempted to think that your dreams are not good enough simply because others are seemingly doing better. The best way to do that is to understand that every individual has their own life purpose and interests, and you have your own for a reason. Therefore, do not compare yourself to others. Do the best you can to be the best you can be.

Forgive yourself – understand that it is natural to make mistakes. Forgive yourself for making them, learn and keep on going forward.

Let go of the past – no matter what happens, you matter. Your failures, losses, and mistakes do not define you. If you have been given another chance, do not spend it regretting the things of the past or daydreaming about what could have been. Fix up, live and love life.

Cultivate An Attitude of Peace and Calm

Peace! just hearing the word itself sends out incredible much-needed vibrations around and within us. All creation, all of humanity need peace, but how can one attain this noble virtue which can make our lives so much more enjoyable and fulfilling?

Peace is a serene state of being. It is an attitude and culture one can actively cultivate. It does not automatically exist. The moment people wake up, a rush of thoughts plunging them into worry and restlessness often attacks them. Just checking our phones and switching on the television set introduces us to the reality of the hurting world we are living in day today. Amidst the inevitable storms of this life, how can one manage to attain peace and be grounded, not constantly being tossed about by the waves of unforeseen challenging events that await humanity every day?

Attitude of peace

In simple terms, attitude is a way of behaving, feeling, or acting towards a certain person or situation. When undeveloped and immature, the usual way of reacting towards our surroundings is often instinctive or impulsive. Whenever anyone wrongs you, or things do not go as expected, it's often easy to just immediately react negatively with feelings of resentment, bitterness, anger, frustration, and impatience. This is usually the norm when an individual has not trained one's mind to be mindfully responsive rather than instinctively reactive. Always reacting to things that happen to you on a day-to-day basis in that untrained way can most certainly lead one to have a heavy burden to carry all the time no matter where you go.

We are what we think, say, and do

To successfully adapt to our environment and overcome any setbacks that come our way, it is important to consciously decide to cultivate an attitude of peace. This means one must start mindfully training themselves to cultivate a peaceful way of thinking, acting, and speaking. If you had gotten used to the attitude of cultivating the ABC mindset, then that becomes who you become. ABC mindset stands for Accusing Blaming and Complaining. Our repeated thoughts, actions, and words form our habits and ultimately our character. Hence it is possible to unlearn negative reactive behavioral patterns and reprogram ourselves to being a peaceful person by cultivating thoughts, actions, and words that show an attitude of peace. Actively start practicing a culture of peace in how you behave to enjoy the fruit of peace. Practice certainly makes perfect.

Be open-minded to new or different perspectives

Albert Einstein once said, "There are only two ways to live your life, one is as though nothing is a miracle and the other is as though everything is." Decoding everything that happens to you in a negative light robs you of the much-needed peace you could be cultivating and enjoying with others in your sphere of influence. Focus on the positive.

It is better to light a candle than curse the darkness- Chinese Proverb

Most people often have the urge to point out the shortcomings and faults in a system, person, or situation. This often leads to tension, misunderstanding, fights, wrong perceptions, and unintended hurt. Before you know it, the situation would have escalated from bad to worse. Hence to introduce any suggested ways of handling things more fruitfully, it is important to learn to cultivate an attitude of peace in dealing with those situations.

Instead of exposing and calling out shortcomings, a better approach to try first is usually becoming the change you want to see. Through showing a good example of how things should be without making others feel demeaned for not doing it right, you can peacefully introduce positive change which will be gracefully accepted. However, when you try to change things from a place of wrath, frustration, and anger, this closes people's hearts from cooperating willingly and peacefully with you. Which in turn often leads to more negative and strained relations. Therefore, developing an attitude of peace is key to progress.

Acknowledge the other person's reality.

Misunderstandings, strife, and broken relationships often prevail when we resist acknowledging and respecting other people's perspectives which differ from our own. Learning to communicate peacefully through positive dialogue to settle disputes or differences is key to attaining peaceful co-existence with others and developing authentic peaceful friendly relations. Without mindfully cultivating this attitude of peace it is almost impossible to have peace.

Calm Morning

One of the most beautiful things to witness every day is the gift of waking up to a fresh new day filled with a calm breeze, rays of light radiating from the sun ready to illuminate our planet. Waking up to hearing the peaceful calming songs of happy birds always carefree and ready to take on the world. Such a calm morning state that nature presents to us is a blessing we ought to learn to behold and appreciate.

Calm morning routine

Mornings are very important. How they unfold often sets the tone for how the rest of our day will most likely turn out. We are more productive when we are calm, our environment is well organized and our thoughts are also organized. Most chaotic mornings are often due to lack of planning the night before, sleeping too late, waking up to a messy environment, waking up late. Hence to cultivate an attitude of peace and calm morning, many good habits can be practiced to get there. These include having a good rest, not going to bed before resolving any previous conflicts, setting an alarm, starting your day with prayer, meditation, and a glass of warm water before eating anything, just to name a few. Peace is possible, all we need to do is be the change we want to see.

How To Develop Inner Tranquility

Serenity is every 'normal' person's dream. But if you asked me about anything related to it a couple of years ago, I would never have known how to answer adequately. It was only when something huge hit me in recent years that I understood the value of mental health and inner peace. I was left with no other choice but to survive. After trying every trick, I could think of, I realized that the way I felt had more to do with my mindset than anything else. I had to change the narrative that was replaying over again in my head, and I can tell you that power was born the day I made that decision.

I must say though, mental issues are not the easiest to deal with. It takes time for many people to come to terms with various situations or life experiences and be at peace. Whatever the reason you are reading this, remember that you owe yourself a great life and it begins with inner peace. Developing it is up to you.

Why is it important to develop inner tranquility?

It is just unfortunate that life can never be perfect and we sometimes find ourselves in situations we absolutely have no clue how we got into. Sometimes we have dreams but things just do not go according to plan. Even then, someone who has learned how to develop and maintain inner peace will find a way to keep themselves from losing their mind. You learn to enjoy life through it all or accept situations that would otherwise break you. Inner tranquility is like medicine to the soul. Not only does it shield you from being hurt by others. It also shields you from hurting yourself. Having it means that you are mentally stable and can approach situations with positivity. However, this does not mean you do not experience anxiety and the likes. You just know how to keep it from consuming you.

You can use the following tips to develop inner tranquility

1.   Feed your mind positivity – do not entertain negative thoughts and do not pay attention to negative words. Be careful what you listen to read and watch. Those are the things we

often use to form opinions about ourselves and the world around us.

2.   Keep good company – surround yourself with positive and supportive people who will help you push forward. This does not mean you have to find perfect people because you will never meet such. You need people who will be there for you in good and bad times. Sometimes they will forget the same words they used to help you find strength and will need you to repeat the same words to them. As you do that, you are affirming those words and engraving them into your heart.

3.   Stop comparing yourself to others – admiring others and learning from them is good. Just do not compare yourself to them. It could make you feel like your dreams are delaying or you have failed, among other things. It can also make enemies for you and divert you from the right path due to the pressure to do better than the next person.

4.   Let go of the past – your past mistakes and all the disappointments-let them go. Holding on to things you cannot change only serves as a reminder of the pain you have experienced and keeps you reliving that painful experience. Many a time, there are no benefits at all. Give your current life and your dreams the much-needed attention so much that you won't have time to revisit your past.

5.   Do not make everything about you – you are not the center of everything that happens under the sun. You should understand that. What affects you affects others too. Try to

listen to other people and be understanding. This will help you also understand that even the bad things others say about you and their attitude have nothing to do with the person you are or what you are doing. People have their own problems and weaknesses. Therefore, at some point, you will be a victim of uncontrolled emotions arising from those problems and weaknesses. Do not let others define you and do not give room to their negativity.

6.   Celebrate all your victories – appreciate all your wins including the smallest ones. It will help you realize that your life has not only been a series of misfortunes and lack. This can give you hope when going through difficult times and doubt.

7.   Whatever your hands find to do, do it with all your heart – do your best in all your duties. This will keep you from regretting missed opportunities and wasting chances.

8.   Be easy on yourself – forgive yourself, do not put yourself under pressure, and get some rest. They say slow and steady wins a race.

How To Wake Up Peacefully in The Morning

I believe sleep is like a therapy session. When we get in a sort of loop to unbuckle all the days' frustrations and trauma. Time to check out from reality. Just like a restart button to prepare us for tomorrow. When I wake up the following day, I expect to be both mentally and physically awakened. This will give me the right attitude to go through the rest of my day. In meditation, they usually say how one wakes up is a significant factor in deciding how one goes through the day. A famous Indian author also shared some wisdom on how one can wake up in the morning feeling fresh and energized. His enlightenment was that it is not really about the hours of sleep or the sleep quality. It is our quality of living that determines how peaceful we are feeling each morning rise. He advised that we focus more on enhancing our quality of life only then do we increase the quality of sleep we have. When we work hard and take care of our health, we sleep better at night. Appreciating life, exercising, and creating good pre-bedtime routines also affect how peacefully we will feel waking up in the morning.

Appreciate life

So often we tend to take life for granted. We start leaving as if the next day is guaranteed to us. But it is not. Life itself is a gift. The more we get to understand it, we start appreciating it more. Now when we appreciate life, we look at each morning with a different lens of understanding. In such a perspective, we learn to smile with gratitude as we open our eyes to each new day. We are not waking up to headaches of what is lacking in our lives, or what is not, but we're living in the moment with gratitude to what's already there. We should appreciate life more for us to have more peaceful mornings.

Monitor your nighttime routines

Everything we do before bedtime determines the quality of sleep we will have. Drinking too much water before bed will give us many trips to the bathroom during the night. This will affect our sleep cycle and have us feeling not well-rested in the morning. Certain foods take more time to be digested. To avoid feeling bloated and suffering from heartburn whilst disrupting our beauty sleep, it is best advised to eat 4-5 hours before going to bed. Taking caffeinated drinks before bed increases our brain activity. This will keep us tossing and turning for hours after turning the lights off. Smoking is also to be avoided because of nicotine which increases heart alertness. Moreover, taking a shower before bed helps increase our quality of sleep. The bedroom's atmosphere or environment can induce better sleep. Sleeping in a cool, quiet, darkroom, and a comfortable bed is ideal. Even the color of the bedroom walls is crucial. An hour before bedtime, we should try to do something relaxing. Toxic habits such as falling asleep on the phone or in front of the Tv triggers insomniac behavior. This can alter ones' sleep patterns.

Stop hitting the snooze

Waking up gradually to natural light could be a preferred alternative to using an alarm clock. When certainly most people would struggle to do without this tool, it has been found that the device has its shortcomings. In some cases, waking up to an alarm clock inflicts sleep anxiety, a rise in blood pressure, heart rate, and even stress levels. The anticipation and worry not to miss a '5 am alarm' could promote insomnia. Now instead of having a good nights' sleep and waking up on time, you will wake up with an adrenaline rush and panic attack. Do not hit the snooze button. The longer we stay in bed falling in and out of sleep, the more exhausted we will feel once we get up.

Imagine a scenario where you decide to hit the snooze button a couple of times in the morning. Five days later you then decide you need to wake up on that first alarm sound. In this case, the brain gets confused because you have already disrupted your sleep cycle. You are jumping in and out of your sleep cycle. You could drift off into the first stage of sleep and that is the worst time to wake up and that can leave the body in shock. This is known as 'sleep inertia' which causes that familiar feeling of drowsiness after you wake up. Rather, we should try and wake up at the same time every day naturally.

Exercise and Stretch regularly

Exercising and stretching in the morning is a great way to get us rejuvenated and awake. Regular exercise impacts the release of certain chemicals in our bodies. An increase in Serotonin levels stimulates the brain, activates our vitals, and as well improves our appetite. When we exercise our bodies release dopamine and endorphins in our brains that make us feel happy. Stretching too loosens the muscles.

Comprehensively to keep having more peaceful mornings, let us first attain inner peace. In Viggo Mortensen's words, "One of the best pieces of advice I ever got was from a horse master. He told me to go slow to go fast." I think that applies to everything in life. We live as though there are not enough hours in the day but if we do each thing calmly, we will get it done quicker and with much less stress.

It is not stress that kills us, it is our reaction to it. - Hans Selye.

Introspection: The Key to Inner Peace

Many people believe that inner peace is a myth. Maybe that is because in the actual world, there is too much noise around for one to meditate or engage in activities that modern media advocates for when seeking peace. They all seem like a luxury we cannot afford to spare time for. We are in a hurry to achieve after all.

Yet, if we are not deliberate about discovering tranquility, we risk being swallowed up by the busyness of life. If we are not active about bringing calm to the world where 'fast' is the order of the day and patience is scarce, do we not become vulnerable to frustration and stress?

Peace is the greatest response we can have to situations that put pressure on us. It is the way we maintain sanity amid chaos. Through peace, we bring calm to circumstances that call for frustration.

Unfortunately, the external environment that confronts us today is too chaotic to bring peace without participation from within us. When you turn on the news, the headlines do not encourage any sense of calm. Neither does social media with its superficiality. Add the stress of the different workspaces we are part of and the inevitable clashes with well-intending loved ones, and you realize that there is little hope for peace to come from outside.

We are our own sources of peace because we can build it from inside. While we have external agents that encourage peace- such as a healthy working environment or supportive social connections- true peace is something that we nurture within. We draw it out when we come across situations that try our patience. It is inner peace that allows you to walk away from a clash with your impossible boss, or that holds you back when you would rather engage in a screaming match with a spouse or family member. Inner peace keeps you from being buried alive by hardships. It allows you to draw on calm when you would rather resort to the default human reaction of anger, frustration or worry.

Introspection plays a huge role in bringing peace.

To introspect is to take a journey within yourself to discover a lot about what makes you who you are. When you examine yourself and how you deal with stressful situations, it helps you control your emotions and your reactions. Introspection offers you the opportunity to discover what triggers panic and uncertainty, and what makes you calm.

'Developing clarity within yourself improves self-assessment, decision-making, and overall happiness. Rather than reacting in the heat of the moment, you can act with understanding, calm, and wisdom.' G. Razzetti.

We play a role in every adverse situation we encounter. Sometimes, we are even to blame because of our actions or lack thereof. Often, we may even be unaware that we are creating sticky situations that will haunt us later. Other times, we are victims of the actions of others. Either way, we are participants who either contribute to the situation or react to it. Introspection allows us to step away and examine the part we play.

Let us say that you clash with your boss over a misunderstanding. The default reaction is to go on the defensive and point out that your boss was not paying attention. Your boss may feel you are challenging them, and it escalates into an argument. When you draw on your inner peace and introspect, you may well discover that you could have done better to give a clearer picture to prevent any misunderstanding. That is not to admit guilt for something your boss may genuinely have failed to understand. It is to examine whether you could have played a role in avoiding the misunderstanding. That interpretation can bring calm to a tense situation as it allows you to respond differently to the scenario.

Introspection is not embarking on a fault-finding mission for every difficult situation you find yourself in. It examines not only the bad but allows you to look at your successes and your contribution to positive situations in your life. Peace can also come from knowing that you are doing your best. You find motivation to do better from positive reflections too.

Introspection means noticing more of my inner world, especially as it reacts and responds to external stimulus, whether good or bad. The emphasis on introspection during negative circumstances just helps us approach adversity more calmly and allows us to cultivate inner peace in situations that call for the opposite. The decisions you make are based on your approach to hardships, regardless of who authored the mess. Introspection is just a unique approach that allows you to examine whether you can avoid escalation of a situation by being kinder and more compassionate to yourself or to others.

Asking yourself hard, introspective questions about a situation you find yourself in will allow you to think before you act or speak. It will save you from having to explain yourself after saying the wrong thing in the heat of the moment. It will keep you from condemning yourself or others over mistakes. The practice of regular introspection will nurture peace in any environment, no matter how hostile it seems.

How to engage in introspection.

•   Find a quiet space to reflect. Somewhere that allows you to think without interruption. You could even take a short walk to the park.

•   Ask yourself hard questions about your thoughts, feelings and responses to certain scenarios. Pause and thoroughly think them through.

•   Write your answers down. Be honest. Capturing your responses helps you evaluate your own thoughts or feelings.

- Study your responses and draw a conclusion about your character or your behavior in the different circumstances you reflect on.

- Make a commitment to improve where you need to.

Peace is internal, so you can cultivate it by becoming more self-aware. It is time we spend understanding our thoughts that allows us to control our response to situations, no matter how negative they are.

No One Else Is Responsible for Your Happiness

Happiness continues to elude many people, not because it does not exist but because they look to the wrong source. Disappointment follows on the heels of every expectation you put on another person or object to make you happy. Peace comes from knowing that you are the only true source of your happiness.

'The greater part of our happiness and our misery depends upon our disposition and not upon our circumstances.' Martha Washington.

We cannot limit happiness to an emotion that we experience when things are going well. Instead, it is a state of mind that we can adopt. One must choose to pursue it through their actions. You could go through some of the most troublesome times in your life and still choose to be happy through it all. It does not mean that sadness does not creep in or that you perpetually smile through the pain. Neither does it mean that a state of happiness vanquishes trouble or that overwhelming sense of defeat we sometimes encounter. Happiness is making the most of every season in your life and choosing to find the positive in the surrounding chaos.

Losing your job will not encourage positivity. There are bills to pay and people to take care of. An option would be to cry at the unfairness of the situation. It does not solve the problem, though. The more you allow negativity to creep in through worry and anxiety, the more the situation seems unbearable. It affects your mental health and your relationships.

Another option would be to see the loss as a state of transition between opportunities. You could use that time to evaluate your skills and upgrade them so that better opportunities find you well prepared. You can also use that time to follow through on that business idea and look for potential partners and investors. It could be a season to investigate your gifts and talents to start an income-generating project. It is all in the way you choose to perceive it.

You are ultimately responsible for any state you choose to be in, even after life throws you curveballs.

Giving such responsibility to another person or material things is to give them too much control over you. To let someone else be your source of happiness is to depend on them. They get to decide when you are happy. You do not want another person dictating how often you are happy, otherwise, you may never experience true happiness in your lifetime. Neither do you want happiness determined by material possessions as the world dictates today.

Our definition of happiness differs from that of the next person. This is because it is intrinsic. It stems from our internal makeup and what we value. So, if another person sees value in something that you do not, already there is potential that you will not be happy with what they choose to prioritize. This is why you should choose happiness on your terms, not on someone else's. The reason people are so unhappy today is that they continue to look to their friends, family, spouses, or careers for happiness. When these things cannot fill that void, people see a life of doom and misery.

If you want to experience true peace, define what makes you happy and make it your responsibility to bring that happiness to your sphere.

Taking responsibility for your own happiness.

Know what makes you truly happy.

No one knows you better than you. The more time you spend with yourself, the more you get to know what you enjoy doing and what brings you joy. If you do not make these important discoveries about these triggers, you will get swept up in other people's happiness, doing what makes them happy while never achieving that same state.

Do not try so hard to fit in.

Many people struggle so much with the need for acceptance and validation from society. We want to blend in so much that we sacrifice our happiness for a seat at the table. It is frustrating to pretend to be someone else and to force yourself to like what they like. Do not shortchange yourself. Be true to your identity. You will be happier existing as your true, undiluted self. If other people dislike what you bring, find another table with those who appreciate you for who you are.

Never compare your life to someone else's.

The greatest source of dissatisfaction and unhappiness is the perception that someone else has it better than we do. When we look to the other side and see their greener grass, we become unsettled about our own lives. There is nothing wrong with looking on the other side for inspiration. Success stories should fuel us to work harder after all. The problem comes when jealousy takes the place of admiration. Accept where you are in life. It is the right place to be at that moment, especially if you are working hard to improve yourself. You need the rags to bear witness to your journey to riches. Your turn will come. Be content in the place you are now.

Be grateful.

Gratitude is a state of mind that allows us to appreciate what we have. While we may desire better, gratitude allows us to look at what relationships and opportunities we have as a blessing that others may not have. To cultivate happiness in difficult moments, consider what you have and be thankful for it. An attitude of gratitude is an important ingredient of happiness.

We cannot avoid tough seasons in our lives. Things may not always go according to plan, and that is okay. When we take full responsibility for our happiness, we control the narrative of the lives we live. Do not give anyone control by making them responsible for what makes you happy. It is a burden only you should bear because no one knows what makes you happy better than you.

Peace Affirmations That Work

'We have to retrain our thinking and speaking into positive patterns if we want to change our lives.' Louise Hay.

Peace is a state of mind more than anything. It is about keeping a calm and stress-free internal environment. When you face challenges and remain level-headed and calm as opposed to angry and frustrated, you have attained that serene state of mind.

The mind is where we fight most wars that determine our thoughts, mood, actions and our behavior. Our nature turns to negative scenarios much quicker than it embraces positivity. To overcome this flaw of humanity, we must constantly fight off negativity and replace it with a positive mindset. It is the only way to calm the noise. It is the only way to attain peace.

Affirmations are a great way to condition our minds for positivity. Just like daily physical activities help condition the body for health, affirmations do the same for the mind. Positive thinking is a phenomenon that seeks to do away with negative thoughts. Unfortunately, as great as that would be, it is not always possible to stop yourself from having bad thoughts. Life will always come with challenges, and such negative thoughts will creep in without us being aware. Hence the bad moods we engage in now and then. To get positive thoughts to wash out the negativity, one can use affirmations.

When you recite affirmations, it is the same as having a pep talk.

Before a team goes out to play, the coach or captain gathers them together and gives a type of motivational speech. As players engage in whatever sporting discipline, they replay that speech in their heads, and it gives them the leverage they need to do their best. That speech empowers them and makes them feel like they can achieve victory against their opponents.

Affirmations are forms of positive self-talk that help your mind to embrace a different perspective around a certain area. The beauty of affirmations is you are the one giving yourself that empowering talk. The more you tell yourself that you are brave or that you can do whatever you set your mind to do, the more believable it becomes. You can use affirmations in any arena of your life. The results are always positive, but only if you are consistent to do it as often as you can.

Peace and affirmations.

The environment we live in does not always encourage peace. Too much is the hands of other people who may not share the same values and ethics or moral code as us. You can try to influence all those different environments to be calm by practicing the virtues that relate to peace. It may not always work, however. Conflicts will always arise. In such moments, you can make your own personal space a place of tranquility. You do not have to give in to negative thoughts and situations.

Use daily affirmations to condition your mind for peace. It may start off strange that you can speak peace into existence, but it becomes believable with practice. Calling upon that peace during stressful moments will keep you from being swept under by the tides of life.

You can choose to do your peace affirmations during a specific time of the day, one that allows you to absorb what you are saying in a serene environment. Other people swear by early morning affirmations. It makes sense because it sets the tone for the day before you encounter anything that can threaten that peace. Handling difficult clients or dealing with your work or school pressure becomes bearable after spending your quiet time conditioning your mind for peace.

How to come up with personal affirmations.

Affirmations open the door to positivity. The good thing about them is that you can come up with your own affirmations of peace, based on what you want to change or influence in your different environments. Because affirmations are like a pep talk, you can author statements that speak peace into the spheres you want. You can come up with phrases that your mind can believe. It does not have to be a complex, other-worldly statement that showcases your poetic ability. You can write affirmations in a language that your mind understands. The simplest and shortest affirmations can do the trick.

Here are some examples of peace affirmations that work:

1   My mind is a haven of peace.

2   I am at peace with myself and with my environment.

3   I am at peace with others, even those who are not at peace with me.

4   I choose to be calm.

5   I am a beacon of peace to all the people I encounter.

6   I choose to have a peaceful day.

7   Peace is my first response to adversity.

8   Nothing can take away my inner peace.

9   I release all the negative energy that threatens to disturb my peace.

10   I handle every situation and every event with calmness and self-control.

11   I think peaceful thoughts and enjoy peace in my life.

Affirmations are like nutrients that enrich the soil of our minds. Whatever we plant grows because the soil is rich. The more you choose to think thoughts that make you feel at peace, the quicker the affirmations work.

If you want to change your approach to negative circumstances that threaten your inner peace, use affirmations. They will bring calm to any situation.

Say NO to Some Things

Not everything that we are interested in doing is good for us and that makes it hard to decide what to say yes or no to. We often buckle under the pressure of societal norms and we say yes to things we have no interest in, some of us have no idea who we are because we dishonor ourselves and say yes to everything that comes our way. No is a powerful word and it is a complete sentence that does not need to be defended. You are well within your rights to say NO! You need to say yes to living the life of your dreams.

Being a good person is something we all strive to be, we want the people who are in our lives to look at us and be pleased with what they see so we say yes. Yes to hanging out, taking that leap, lending them money, listening to them, the list is endless. We say yes so much to the point that it becomes an automated response. There comes a time when all the yes's we dish out leave us worn out. You have no time for yourself and the things that you love, when giving to the cause of friendship begins to deplete your energy this is when you realize that it is important to say no. While saying no may seem selfish it is an act of self-love and it will give you time to focus on yourself. It is important to take care of number one because you cannot pour from an empty cup. If you struggle with saying no here are some things to consider if your default setting has become yes.

Say NO to things that do not honor who you are.

TD Jakes says that if you know who you are, then you know who you are not. If you don't know who you are, somebody can ascribe any identity onto you and you will morph into whoever they expect you to be. Honoring yourself entails being honest with yourself, it includes saying no to things that do not bring you joy or you simply are not interested in doing. Do not allow the need to be liked by people and have their approval be what you make your decisions based on, suppressing your needs and self-sacrificing does not honor you in any way. Your loved ones deserve to have you show up for them because you truly care for them and you want to spend time with them. The version of you that reluctantly says yes and wishes to be elsewhere will only lead to resentment, dragging yourself along and forcing yourself to have fun leads to inauthentic connections in your life and you deserve better than that.

Say NO to things that do not bring you peace.

Peace should be a big factor when deciding on saying yes or no. You should say yes to things that will allow you to have peace of mind, yes to things that will rejuvenate your soul, and things that make you happy. Everything that you need to think about and have to convince yourself to do because you are aware that it will drain your energy you must say no. For your peace of mind and sanity you must simply learn to say no. Constantly saying yes leads to people expecting us to constantly go out of our way to show up for them, and they expect you to place their needs above yours. In the long run, this causes strain on relationships and you regret having been there for your loved ones. As you say yes or no, remember that you teaching people how to treat you and you want people to treat you with kindness and respect because you stand up for yourself.

Understand that NO is a complete sentence.

Often, we feel bad and we feel guilty when we say no to our loved ones. We will begin with an apology; I am sorry but I am going to have to say no. We feel the need to soften the blow and it doesn't matter how softened the blow is but we will feel bad as soon as no leaves our mouths. We feel like saying no to our loved ones is such a letdown and we need to justify ourselves for having the audacity to say no. The truth of the matter is that no is a complete sentence and you are allowed to just say no. You need to have confidence in your no and surround yourself with people that are aware that saying no to them is saying yes to yourself.

Saying no is you practicing self-love. You do not always need to be available to everyone for everything, take time out and focus on yourself. Say yes to a day of relaxation and rejuvenation, say yes to spending time alone, say yes to missing out on dinner plans, and say yes to YOU. You deserve to say yes to yourself. Keep in mind that as you try to nurture relationships with other people you should never forget about the lifelong relationship you can never escape which is a relationship with yourself. Stop making up negative scenarios of what might happen if you say no and remember that other people's reactions have nothing to do with you.

Stop Worrying About What Others Think

Whether we do good or bad, people will always talk; what matters the most is what you choose to listen to and why you choose to listen to it. Basing our decision-making on what people will say is no way to live because that means you can easily be swayed. We all want to be considerate; we want to make our loved ones proud and happy and we do not want to be known as selfish but where do we draw the line. We sacrifice so much and miss out on life because other people's opinions about our lives matter. Think of all the things you have wanted to do but you never got around to doing because of the fear of being judged and having people talk about you. Do you and stop worrying about what others think of you.

Doing you sounds easy on paper but for it to work you need to know who YOU are. The you that is an individual and not affected by groupthink, the you that is passionate about being alive and living life on your terms. You need to be able to define who you are and what you think your purpose is in the world to be able to cancel out the noise that comes from other people. Once you know exactly who you are and what you want out of life it becomes easy to do you. If you listen to everyone's opinion of who you are supposed to be you will drown in the river of confusion that becomes your life. On the journey to doing you, you will need to look into why other people's opinions have a hold over you. Introspection will shed light on why you do not want to be your person, it will bring to light the co-dependence and all the things that you are afraid to face.

We all want to be there for our loved ones, we want to be called a good friend, sister, or partner and we dishonor ourselves for our loved ones. We forget about the resentment that comes with trying to please everyone but ourselves. We forget about the regret that follows and how that will rob us of peace of mind. We spend so much time focusing on the external noise that is constantly telling us what needs to be done and we forget about the internal roar that we notice when it is too late. The problem with focusing on the external noise is you forget about yourself. You forget about your needs and wants and what you should be doing with your life. What you then get is external noise and no peace when you are on your own because you are neglecting yourself.

Peace. That is the price we pay for forgetting about ourselves and focusing on other people's opinions of us. Many of us are not even familiar with what peace is because we have never experienced it. From the time we are teenagers we want to fit in, we want people to accept us and we do what is necessary to fit in. We move in packs being the social beings that we are and we try to follow the status quo. We toe the line and often the opinions of other people are what will imprison us. Liberation from these prisons is what we need to free ourselves from. The price we pay for peace is to simply be our most authentic selves and doing that which we wish to do. When we focus on ourselves, we break the cycle of turning into the people whose opinions imprison other people.

People that spend their time worrying about what others think of them become people that talk about other people. When you spend your time people-pleasing and you do not live your life people that live their own lives are what you focus on. Then you begin to judge people for doing that which you failed to do, which is to live life on their own terms. People that are courageous enough to take up space in the world and do what matters to them are a bother to you and you talk about them.

How dare they go against the grain and forge their paths. You look at these people with contempt.

The cycle must be broken. We must all focus on living our lives and free other people from our opinions. Spend time doing what you love with people that you care about and do not become a stumbling block in other people's journey. To aspire to live a peaceful and to mind your own business, that should be your motto in life. Focus on your own life and ensure that the loudest voice in your life is your voice.

The Benefits of Using Peaceful Language

The one thing people often struggle to do is giving themselves time to think deeply about what they are about to say especially when they feel provoked. The world has normalized being mean to others, especially on social media. Others claim it is because they have the right to speak their mind while others do it for fame. Almost everyone has uttered unkind words to others for what they thought was a justifiable reason. Often, there is no regard to what this means or does to the person on the receiving end.

Just think about it; you are rushing to an interview and a 'careless stranger' spills his or her coffee on you, or you are waiting for your order but the person responsible has seemingly forgotten and you have watched while s/he served five other people who came after you. Would you remain calm and wait for tomorrow to let such people know how you feel? You may never even get that chance and it certainly would feel like by being easy on the person you are letting him or her get away with it.

The normal thing to do in similar situations would be to scream at the person or let them know how much of an inconvenience they are. Yes, we often feel people deserve it and they need to be taught a lesson. Sometimes it is just about the pressure to prove that we are not weak. But, what difference does it make? Does it change what has already happened to you? Isn't there a way of teaching them a lesson other than screaming and being mean? How would you prefer someone you've wronged to talk to you? And, what if you choose peace?

Below are the benefits of taking your time to choose the right words;

1.   It promotes peace – when you choose to use peaceful language, you shun a possible war. Even someone who was expecting you to retaliate so that they can escalate their issues with you is denied that opportunity. You never know what the other person would have said next would have done to you.

2.   You do not ruin things – sometimes our choice of words ruins things that would have otherwise been perfect. Some words cannot be taken back and the results cannot be fixed. In a

world where misunderstandings and miscommunications occur, it is crucial to ensure that you calmly communicate and seek understanding before you lash out unnecessarily. This could mess up your relationships and reputation for good. Try and remember this every time you are angry or disappointed. Calm down before you can attempt to discuss issues with your employer or spouse.

3.   You create an environment that is conducive for proper discussion – using peaceful words makes it easier to talk issues out with people where harsh words would make them defend themselves and 'fight back'. It is, therefore, easier to find solutions to problems or have a meaningful discussion when the involved parties choose peace and respect. Do not let pride take control of the situation.

4.   You easily create and maintain meaningful relationships – people respect those who show respect. Your choice of words is part of the criteria spectators will use when choosing whether to associate with you. This is true also in forming friendships in your social life or teams in the work environment. Also, people will most likely want to be associated with you because they respect and admire you not because they are scared to ever be thought of as your rivalry.

5.   You save others from hurt and stress – so many people who doubt themselves and think of their lives as worthless are victims of verbal abuse. Unfortunately, some have even lost their lives to that. You may think you are teaching people a lesson or making them stronger (where a parent and a child are involved) when you are actually driving them into a dark space.

With the way people are facing mental health issues some of which are kept secret, choose your words as though everyone is a patient.

6.   Your intentions can be better understood – it is easier to be understood when you use peaceful language than when you are harsh or mean. For example, there are times when we need to compliment others for a job well done or congratulate them on their achievements but at the same time point out an issue or two that they need to fix or guard against. If we do not choose our words carefully in such cases we can easily come across as jealous. It won't matter that the attempts are from a good place.

7.   It could be your shield in future – we all make mistakes, have bad days, or work under pressure. You might, one day, be the one spilling coffee on the same person or taking forever to serve a client due to pressure. If you are known to be forgiving, understanding, and gentle, any normal person would understand and forgive your mistakes too without using hurtful words.

Get Rid of Regrets

Peace is a beautiful thing. There is nothing as satisfying as being at peace with yourself and the decisions that you would have made. However, regrets have a way of snatching that peace right from under us and breeding life of torment and suffering. Regrets usually seep in when we go over our lives and our day and we begin to analyze the decisions that we would have made and we realize that some may not have been the best decisions, and some decisions would have been made a while back and years have gone by but that gnawing feeling will not leave you alone. "I should/not have..." the statement we all say to ourselves sometimes and that steals our joy and peace. To live a peaceful life, regrets must be done away with, it is not an easy process but one that can be done.

Make amends.

We all say things we do not mean or do things we should not at some point one way or another. However, if there is a chance to make amends for the thing that you regret, this is the simplest way to get rid of regrets. We have been there whereas a parent you yell at your child unnecessarily, and the guilt and the regret start eating at you. The best way out of the situation is to make amends. Making amends allows you to see things from that person's perspective and one can be forgiven and sometimes one may not be forgiven, but the fact that you owned up and tried to make amends may bring you peace.

Regret is not only in how we treat people but also in the opportunities that we let go of. You are offered an opportunity but because at the moment it did not seem right for you but now you are stuck and you are regretting not taking it up. Call up that person, email that organization and make amends, you may get a second chance. The challenge most of us face is that we shy away from making amends because it is embarrassing, or that it seems like we are begging and it is somewhat beneath us. This is the reason regrets go on for so long, simply because we will not choose to try and make amends while the situation is permitting for the sake of peace.

The past belongs in the past, but the future is yours to have

Making amends is great but only when the situation permits. Some situations are either too far gone or there is no way to make right no matter what efforts are put into trying to make them right. The best way to get peace and get rid of regrets is to leave the past right where it belongs, in the past. Make an effort to move on with your life the best way your know-how. Look for other opportunities, meet other people and work on those things. Rehashing the past will not in any way change it, it will just frustrate you more, thus it is better to leave things as they are, and forge a new path going forward. Regrets are usually a thing of the past. The best way to let them go is to focus on the here and the now. Living in the present means actively living out your best life despite the things that would have happened in the past. Being at peace or choosing peace does not mean that you do not feel bad enough if it concerns something that you did and regret. Choosing peace means you are willing to give yourself another chance at life and not allowing what you did to steal your joy. This does not negate that you feel awful about your actions, it does not mean that you do not seek forgiveness, it means that you can still feel awful and seek forgiveness and that you desire a life without regrets.

If you cannot change something, change how you think about it

More often than not, the way we remember things is not always how things would have played out. We remember things according to the emotions we felt, the way we see and view things, our belief systems, and so many other social constructs. Ever been there where an issue gives you sleepless nights until you see that person or call them to apologize and they tell you there is nothing to apologize for because they did not see things the way that you did. Well, this is the same with regrets. You may beat yourself up for making a certain decision yet it was not that big a deal. Thus, my encouragement to change how you look or think about things. Instead of beating yourself up for being human, why not choose to think of yourself in a more kind and forgiving manner, look for the silver lining in the dark cloud. Understand that everything either good or bad happens for a reason, and good or bad is only how you see things. If you saw things differently, the outcome may surprise you.

In closing, peace is good for the soul and we all deserve to live a peaceful life. Part of being human is that we will all make mistakes at one point or another, but punishing yourself by carrying the burden of regret does not help any situation. If there is a chance to make recompense by all means do, if not choose to move forward with your life without the burden of regret. Being regretful is not synonymous with being sorry for your actions or lack thereof, it's a burden that you can put down and still be very remorseful about your actions. So, do what you can to get rid of regrets and get some peace.

The Virtue Of Peacefulness

'The greatest virtues are those which are most useful to other persons.' Aristotle.

Virtues are guidelines of how we should conduct ourselves around others. They shape our character so that we know what makes up good and moral behavior. As many as they are, the world would benefit if we could choose to live by just a handful of them.

One who lives a virtuous life makes a habit of doing all they can to extend goodness to others. Virtues allow us to not only strive to perform good acts, but to give the best of ourselves with every act. World peace would be more achievable if we took it upon ourselves to be more patient, honest, tolerant, accepting and compassionate with others. It would not hurt for us to show a little humility too, for most of the clashes result from pride and ego.

Peacefulness is a virtue. It is an intrinsic quality that can have an external impact on our society and on the world. When we approach every disagreement and misunderstanding with calmness, we avert conflicts. When you respect others, accepting their opinion as valid and tolerating their perspective, you are exercising the virtues of peace. Showing others you understand them and value them despite your differences will always encourage an environment of peace in your interactions with them.

Peace is an inner-state of wellbeing. It starts with you. When you are at peace with yourself, exercising compassion and extending grace to yourself when you make mistakes, you extend that peace to others around you. It becomes easier to keep your composure in difficult situations. You remain calm when the pressures of life threaten to overwhelm you.

The benefits of peacefulness.

Conflict keeps us frustrated and agitated. It does not allow our thoughts and emotions to settle. Peacefulness eases that pressure. When you let go of conflict and the need to pay someone back for their actions against you, it does wonders for your mind.

'Serenity is not freedom from the storm, but peace amid the storm.' Unknown.

Keeping calm allows you to control your reactions to trying situations. Regret always follows after we give in to irrational responses. There is no benefit to resorting to our baser instinct to fight back when someone provokes us. Often, it is difficult to take back harsh words you exchange with someone during a disagreement. More so to reverse the consequences of your actions. A calm approach keeps you from making rash decisions because of anger or frustration.

There are many health issues that are connected to our mental state. Anger and frustration only agitate our minds. This will have an effect on our physical health. When you embrace peace, it reduces the risk of stress-related diseases.

Peacefulness has a direct correlation to happiness. Happy people always make the best out of every situation. They rarely keep grudges or scores for wrong done to them.

Peacefulness in any environment helps you focus on what matters. When a work environment is full of conflict, people will find it difficult to concentrate on their work tasks. Make the workplace a peaceful place and see how productive people can become. The same goes with a peaceful home. Everybody thrives.

How to practice the virtue of peacefulness.

'Between stimulus and response, there is a space. In that space is our power to choose our response. In our response lies our growth and our freedom.' Viktor Frankl.

Our actions towards others during moments of conflict determine whether the outcome will be peace or chaos. Practicing the following will help us exhibit the virtue of peacefulness:

Temperance.

Restraint will be key in conflict situations. When provoked, you are tempted to respond a certain way. Restraint allows you to hold back. Refrain from fanning the flames into an uncontrollable inferno. It will burn bridges you may need in the day of trouble.

Patience.

A patient response to adversity will promote peace. Be patient with others.

Acceptance.

Denial of a situation will not make it go away. When you acknowledge its existence, you deal with it calmly. Denying that there is a problem will harm you because you will not deal with it as you should if you pretend it does not exist. Bad things happen to good people. Not everyone agrees with your views or your methods. You cannot get everyone to like you, no matter how good you are. Embracing all that will bring peace.

Tolerance.

People may have opinions that differ from yours, and that is okay. Convincing them they are wrong to think the way they do will cause unnecessary clashes. When you tolerate them despite their difference to you in terms of values, ethics, race; and you agree to disagree on the fundamentals, you will create harmony. Co-existence does not have to mean seeing eye-to-eye on everything.

Compassion.

The ability to empathize with others as they go through difficulties will keep you from stepping on their toes unnecessarily. Peace comes when you understand others. Piling stress upon them during tough seasons will not bring peace to their world or to yours.

Forgiveness.

Letting go of the hurts of the past will encourage peacefulness. When someone shows remorse for their actions, forgive them and move on. Be willing to reconcile your differences and start on a clean state. Repaying bad for bad done to you will remove the element of peace from the equation.

Kindness.

It costs little to be kind to another person. When someone reaches out for help, and you have the capacity, assist them. It gives you peace knowing that you have made a difference in someone's life.

There is a lot that one can do to bring peace to their world and the world of others around them. It is the virtue of peacefulness which allows us to live in harmony. Play your part and bring calm to a chaotic world. Find peace within you and spread it through your habits and your deeds.

Emerson's words, "Nothing can bring you peace but yourself."

CPSIA information can be obtained
at www.ICGtesting.com
Printed in the USA
BVHW040845020821
613407BV00015B/853